Will Witmer

Colonel Harry Estes

Will Witmer

Colonel Harry Estes

ISBN/EAN: 9783337124496

Printed in Europe, USA, Canada, Australia, Japan

Cover: Foto ©ninafisch / pixelio.de

More available books at **www.hansebooks.com**

COLONEL HARRY ESTES,

Or, From

WEST POINT

—TO—

THE SURRENDER OF LEE.

AN

HISTORICAL AND MILITARY DRAMA WITH ACCOM-
PANYING TABLEAUX, IN SIX ACTS.

By WILL. T. WITMER.

NORWALK, OHIO:
Chronicle Steam Printing Establishment,
1877.

COL. HARRY ESTES,

Or, From

WEST POINT

—TO—

THE SURRENDER OF LEE.

AN

HISTORICAL AND MILITARY DRAMA WITH ACCOM-
PANYING TABLEAUX,

IN SIX ACTS.

By WILL. T. WITMER.

NOTICE.—This play has been duly copyrighted, and every person is cautioned, under the penalties of the law, not to present it without the written consent of the manager. W. T. WITMER, Manager.

NORWALK, OHIO
Chronicle Steam Printing Establishment,
1877.

To Capt. HENRY G. STAHL, of the 3d O. V. C., a soldier, gentleman and scholar, this drama is respectfully dedicated by   THE AUTHOR.

CAST OF CHARACTERS.

HARRY ESTES, Cadet at West Point, afterward Lieutenant-Colonel U. S. Volunteers.

CHARLES HOWE, Cadet at West Point, afterward Colonel C. S. Army.

JONATHAN BUNKER, Sergeant U. S. Volunteers.

GENERAL CORSE, U. S. Volunteers.

MAJOR GRAVES, Cadet at West Point, afterward Major C. S. A.

CAPTAIN HARKNESS, Quartermaster U. S. Volunteers.

COLONEL ANDREWS, Cadet West Point, afterward Col. U. S. A.

CAPTAIN LYKE, Commandant and U. S. Volunteer.

SQUIRE DUNHAM, Justice of Peace at——

BELL, Cadet West Point, afterward Signal Officer.

FOSTER, Cadet West Point, afterward Capt. U. S. Volunteers.

SAM,
JIM, } Contrabands.

TOMMY HALE, Citizen and Orderly U. S. Army.

GENERAL SHERMAN,
GENERAL SLOCUM, } U. S. Army.

CAPTAIN COOKE, Captain C. S. Army.

Soldiers, Officers, Citizens, etc.

LOTTIE HOWE, Sister to Charles Howe.

MAY FULLER, friend of Lottie.

MARIAR BUNKER, wife of Jonathan Bunker.

MRS. DUNHAM, wife of Squire Dunham.

COSTUMES.

HARRY ESTES. First dress, Captain, cadet gray uniform; second dress, Lieutenant-Colonel U. S. Volunteers.

CHARLES HOWE. First dress, cadet uniform; second dress, Col. C. S. Army.

JONATHAN BUNKER. First dress, long linen coat, no vest, dark pants, inside his boots, old sword; second dress, Sergeant U. S. Army.

GENERAL CORSE. General U. S. Army.

MAJOR GRAVES. First dress, cadet; second dress, Major C. S. A.

CAPTAIN COOKE, Captain C. S. A.

CAPTAIN HARKNESS. Captain U. S. A.

COLONEL ANDREWS. First dress, cadet; second dress, Col. U. S. A.

CAPTAIN LYKE. U. S. Volunteers.

SQUIRE DUNHAM. Citizen's dress.

BELL, FOSTER,} First dress, cadet; second dress, Officers U. S. A.

TOMMY HALE. First dress, citizen; second dress, Orderly, U.S.A.

SAM. Gray wig, old clothes.

JIM. Black wig; first, old citizen's clothes; second, old soldier's overcoat and cap.

GENERAL SHERMAN, GENERAL SLOCUM,} General's Uniform.

LOTTIE HOWE. First dress, elegant afternoon dress; second dress, very plain.

MAY FULLER, MARIAR BUNKER,} Very plain.

MRS. DUNHAM. Old lady's dress.

COLONEL HARRY ESTES.

ACT I.

SCENE I.

Interior of Cadet Barracks at West Point—Table with pen, ink, and paper, and two chairs, R. *Cadets* FOSTER *and* ANDREWS *enter at* C. *door, and prepare for dress parade.*

Foster. In a military point of view, perhaps Anderson did right in abandoning Moultrie, but I tell you, Andrews, it will have a bad effect.

Andrews. Why, how is that ?

Foster. It will embolden these Southerners and look very much like weakness on the part of the Government. It's very evident that old Andrew Jackson is not President. The fact is, Andrews, any man who lives to be sixty-five years of age and does not marry a wife, is not fit to be President of the United States any way.

Andrews. Why, Foster, Anderson could not have held Moultrie twelve hours if attacked from the rear; the fortification was never intended to stand an attack from the land, and *I* think Anderson used good judgment in abandoning the fort.

Fos. Well, I tell you the only way to treat an incipient rebellion is to show a bold front, and this bluster will soon cease.

And. There's where *you* make a mistake, Ed; these Southern people mean just what they say. You heard what Peagram and Fitz-Lee said at the riding-hall yesterday?

Fos. Yes, and if we had a loyal officer in command

here, they would have been dismissed from the academy before night.

And. [*Surprised.*] Do you doubt the Superintendent's loyalty?

Fos. [*Laughing.*] No, I don't doubt his loyalty, for he never had any; if he has, it is of that milk-and-water kind they all have.

And. They! whom do you mean by they?

Fos. Why, every officer, almost without exception, in the army of Southern birth.

And. You are wrong, Foster. I am sure, as I said before, these excited people have resolved to fight, but I have a higher opinion of those who have sworn to defend the flag.

Fos. They are all alike, all alike. Some of them would like to be loyal no doubt, but this foolish idea of State allegiance will prove too much for them, and they will all go.

And. What will the Government do with half its army gone?

Fos. Do? I'll tell you what it will do; a Government like ours, to be saved from rebellion, must save itself. Our little army of 18,000 to 20,000 men may serve as a nucleus, but let Anderson be compelled to strike the old flag to Beauregard, and you will see an army springing into life, as if by magic. Yes, sir, from the shop, the counting-room, the pulpit, and the plow, you will see an army gathered; and if this Government can be saved, they will save it. (*Enter Cadet Capt.* ESTES c. *door, as if going to dress parade.*) Estes, Andrews was just intimating to me that the Superintendent favors the South in this movement.

Estes. *   *   *   Well, I believe he does.

Fos. I was just saying so, and to prove it, the band has not played a single national air at parade, since these troubles commenced.

Estes. *   *   *   A national air.

Fos. Yes, that is all very well, but how.

Estes. *   *   *   See that Reming gets it.

Both. Agreed.

Fos. [*Sits at table and writes, reading aloud as he writes.*]

"HEAD-QUARTERS CORPS CADETS,

"U. S. MILITARY ACADEMY, WEST-POINT,

"APRIL 14th, 1861

"The band attached to this corps is hereby directed to play this evening—"

What will we have, boys—Star Spangled Banner?

Estes. * * * Return to barracks.

Fos. [*Finishes by writing and reading.*] "Bandmaster Reming is charged with the execution of this order. By order of——" [*Rising.*] There, Estes, now sign it.

Estes. [*Signs it.*] There she is.

And. [*Taking it.*] If I had not seen you write it, I would have sworn the Superintendent wrote it himself.

Estes. * * * Call will beat off very soon.

[*Exit* ANDREWS c.

Fos. What do you think about Anderson abandoning Moultrie, Estes?

Estes. It was a good move.

Enter GRAVES *and* HOWE *with muskets, full dress, for parade.*

Fos. Well, if I had been in his place I should have staid there till they shelled me out any way. This talk is all very well, but when they come to fire on the old flag, that is another matter.

Graves. What is?

Fos. I say the South will hesitate a long time before they will do that. I want you to understand, gentlemen, that means war.

Howe. And if necessary to preserve our rights, we mean *war* every time.

Estes. * * * To desert his flag?

Graves. Estes, the South by nature are an impulsive people, and the outrages inflicted upon us for the past ten years has goaded us up to so high a pitch that if to secure our rights, we are obliged to inaugurate a war, we will not shrink from the responsibility.

Fos. Those are pretty bold words for a United States cadet.

Graves. I have stated what, in my opinion, they will do. I did not say I approve it.

Howe. Well, I say I approve it. [*To* GRAVES.] And any Georgian who hesitates to say so is no better than a Massachusetts abolitionist.

Graves. I expressed no opinion whatever. If the worst comes to the worst, I may be governed by the requirements of my State.

Estes.   *   *   *   Mounted on alligators.

Enter ANDREWS C. door.

Howe. [*Angrily.*] You can test my courage here and now, if you wish.

Estes.   *   *   *   But it is time for me to go.

[Exit ESTES C. door.

Howe. You Northern men darsen't fight! you are cowards; you haven't got any blood in your ears.

FOSTER and ANDREWS approach him.

Both. What's that.

Graves. [*Interposing.*] Howe, you allow your passion to run away with your judgment and common sense.

Howe. I will allow no man to insult me, sir, and not resent it.

And. Estes did not mean to insult you, man.

Graves. No; that pretty sister of yours he is in love with, shields you from any such attempt on his part, I assure you.

Howe. That is nothing but a West Point flirtation. If my sister should fall in love and marry a Yankee before this affair is settled, I should disown her, and so would her whole family.

Fos. I believe she loves him.

Graves. Of course she loves him; she pretends she came here to witness the examination, but she came on purpose to see him. I tell you she's gone on Estes.

And. Yes, and he loves her too; the only mark of demerit standing against him is for being absent after taps

last night; and you know all about that, Howe, yourself.
Howe. It's all a flirtation in my opinion.
And. Well, when as strict a soldier as he takes such
chances for a woman, make up your mind it's a pretty
serious flirtation.
[*Call is beat outside for dress-parade—all take muskets
and exit, C. door.*]
[*Clear stage—Change.*]

SCENE II.

*Plain at West Point; Ladies and Gentlemen standing at R. 2 E.;
Band plays "Hail Columbia,"off Stage at L. 3 E.; Company of Cadets enter at R. 1 E., in command of ESTES, cross the stage; file left
up the stage, file left across the stage at upper entrance and halt'
dress as if forming the right Company of Battalion; Band ceases to
play; Orders are all given from off left of stage, as if the line extended away off the stage; Band beats off, playing "Star Spangled
Banner;" Parade is dismissed, and the Sergeant [GRAVES] closes
the ranks; Band plays "Yankee Doodle;" HOWE and three others
step out of the ranks.*

Enter ESTES *from* L. 2 E.

Estes. * * What does this mean?
Howe. It means *this!* I never will march again to that
damned Yankee tune.
Estes. Do you refuse?
Howe. Yes; I'll be dismissed first.
Estes. * * Right face! forward march.
[*Sergeant marches them off the stage.*
[LOTTIE *comes to the front and the other ladies and gen-
tlemen go off at R. 4 E.*]
Lottie. Harry! [ESTES *halts.*] I have witnessed this
act of insubordination on the part of my brother, and I am
pained to see it.
Estes. * * as much pained as I am, Lottie.
Lottie. I hope you do not intend to put your threat into
execution. Remember he has the quick temper peculiar
to all our people, and regrets a hasty action as soon as
committed. Harry, he is my brother.

Estes.   *   *   Which is impossible.

Lottie. [*Surprised.*] What! would you disgrace him, myself, and our family bv a dismissal from the academy?

Estes.   *   *   *His fault,* not mine.

Lottie. Remember, too, we are Georgians, and you do not comprehend how we are provoked by you Northern people.

Estes.   *   *   Entertain such feelings toward us.

Lottie. Is it natural we should like a people who inaugurate expeditions like John Brown's, and send them among us to incite our slaves to murder and deeds far worse?

Estes.   *   *   No business here at West Point.

Lottie. Were the South the aggressors, and striving like you, you would think differently then.

Estes. Then would I too be wrong.

Lottie. You certainly do not sympathize with the feeling which is making such progress in the North?

Estes.   *   *   Monster secession.

Lottie. Then would you lend your courage and your sword to subjugate my people?

Estes.   *   *   Belongs to my country.

Lottie. [*Indignant.*] Is this the love you bear us? Have all your protestations come to this, that plighting me your love and vowing you would be to me a life's protector, you would do all this?

Estes. You do not understand——

Lottie. [*Angrily.*] Yes, I do, sir; I understand perfectly. You would be the husband who would vow before high heaven to be a woman's protector, and then at the bidding of a lot of fanatical abolitionists, wantonly slay her people.

Estes.   *   *   Between my duty and my love for you.

Lottie. I believed you loved me; believing which, to you I gave my heart, for you were dearer to me than all the world besides. Our vows are pledged, requiring naught but heaven's approval to make us man and wife. My word s given and I should not ask to make it otherwise;

but to be the wife of him who would invade our home and murder my people—*never.*

Estes.   *   *   Turn my back upon the flag.

Lottie. Sir, I accept your generous offer, and will never be the wife of my people's executioner.

Estes.   *   *   Regretted alike by all.

Lottie. We do not ask your sympathy, sir; we have learned to hate you, and will have a government of our own.

Estes.   *   *   Henceforth our paths lie wide apart.

Lottie. My path, sir, leads me towards my Southern home; It may be one beset with danger, privation and woe. I am a Southern woman, and I shall not hesitate to take it.

Estes.   *   *   If I have loved you——

Lottie. [*Withdrawing her hand.*] You never loved me.

Estes.   *   *   I can not prove a traitor to my country.

Lottie. Then are we to be strangers?

Estes.   *   *   Forsake the old flag, [*hesitatingly*] yes.

Loitie. Then, sir, farewell!

Estes. Farewell! farewell!

[*Exit* LOTTIE *up the stage—exit* ESTES R. 3 E.

[*Change.*]

SCENE III.

SAME AS SCENE I.

Enter Cadets ANDREWS *and* FOSTER, C. *door, from parade, removing hats, muskets, etc.*

Fos. I tell you, Andrews, this affair of Estes and Howe is going to make trouble.

And. Well, so it should. Those fellows ought to be drummed off the Point.

Fos. Do you believe Estes will report them?

And. Why, of course he will; he has got to do it, and unless the Superintendent stands by them, they will be dismissed sure. [*Enter other cadets without arms.*] Let's have a song.

Enter ESTES C. *door.*

Estes. * *   headquarters, gentlemen.

And. [*Aside.*] 1 told you he would report them.

Estes. * *   Have reached a climax at Charleston,

Fos. What of it? Come, let's have the song. Come. some one start her.

[*They sing* "*Benny Havens Oh*"—*Cheers are heard outside.*

Estes. What's that for. [*Enter* BELL, C. *door.*] What is that cheering for, Bell?

Bell. I hurried over to tell you, Sumpter has fallen—has surrendered to Beauregard. Anderson has arrived in New York, and the old flag has been struck to a band of traitors. Howe and the Southern Cadets have got together at Company D.'s barracks and are cheering for Beauregard and the Palmetto flag.

Estes. Boys, will you stand that?

All. No, no, no!

Fos. Let's rally all the men that are true blue, and clean them out.

Estes. Come on.

Bell. Estes, hold on; Howe is the head devil over there, and he swears he will whip you the first time he sees you for reporting him.

Estes. * *   Does that make? Come on.

[*All exit* C. *door.*

[*Change.*]

SCENE IV.

Company D.'s Barrack's—HOWE *and others cheering and singing* "*Bonnie Blue Flag*"—*Guard pacing his beat— Enter* ESTES *and party,* R. 1 E.

Bell. Three cheers for the old flag and an undivided nationality.   [*They cheer.*

Howe. Three cheers for Beauregard and the Southern Confederacy.   [*They cheer.*

Bell. Any man who wears the uniform of a United States Cadet and cheers for that traitor is a traitor himself.

Howe. Whom do you call a traitor?

Bell. Any man who turns his back upon his country.

Estes. * * Clean them out.

[ESTES' *party start to attack—the guard shouts,* "*Turn out the guard*"*—guard turns out, and enter Commandant* LYKE.

Lyke. What does this mean? A riot at West Point.

Bell. It means this, sir, that this academy contains young men who would use its teachings to destroy this Government they have sworn to defend.

Lyke. Every one of you go to your quarters. [*They disperse—guard is dismissed.*] This is shameful. [*Exit* L. 2 E.

[HOWE *and* ESTES *approach each other, followed by a few others.*]

Howe. So you reported me, did you? [ESTES *turns as to go away.*] You Yankee scoundrel! [*Strikes him and knocks him against the wall.*] Now go and report me for that.

[ESTES *rushes toward* HOWE—*the others separate them.*]

Estes. * * Able to whip me.

Howe. That is just what I am.

Estes. * * Stand back and give us a fair show.

ESTES *rushes on* HOWE, *and they fight—finally* ESTES *gets* HOWE *down, and the curtain falls on* ESTES *standing over* HOWE *successful—Tableaux, Secession, on platform in background.*

CURTAIN.

ACT II.

SCENE I.

Exterior Village Hall at——; Men assembled preparatory to a war meeting; Table on lawn at R. U. E. *with pen, ink and paper; Chair for President; Flag hanging over desk; Boys talking to each other: Enter* JONATHAN BUNKER L. 2 E. *with old sword.*

Jonathan. * * Got to come out and fight.

Tom Hale. Bully for Jonathan.

Jon. * * I'm here for the business.

Hale. Yes, I see, Jonathan, you've brought your sword along with you.

Jon.   *   *   Fit with in the Revolution.

Hale. [*Taking it.*] Oh! let's ꜱee it.

[*Others crowd around.*

Jon.   *   *   She's here!

Hale. [*Taking it.*] Oh! hold on, Jonathan, hold on! this is too modern a sword to be Revolutionary. I see it is marked 1812; how's that.

Jon.   *   *   Oh, she's Revolutionary.

Hale. Well, Jonathan, that's a pretty good story and you tell it pretty well, but you can't choke me on it.

[*They all laugh.*

Jon.   *   *   Oh, she's here.

[*Orchestra plays some National air—Enter Squire* DUNHAM *and* ESTES—ESTES, *as a lieutenant-colonel with his arm in a sling.*]

Dunham. [*Taking the chair.*] Gentlemen, allow me to introduce to you Lieutenant-Colonel Estes.

Hale. Three cheers for Colonel Estes.   [*Cheers.*

Dun. Gentlemen, he has authority from the Goverrment to raise a regiment and has come to his native town, where I hope we will not be backward in contributing our proportion of men. You all knew him before he went to West Point. He comes of good patriotic parents; his father was killed at Monterey, after which I adopted Harry, and gave him a West Point education. When the first call was made for troops, he was one of the first to answer. He is a true soldier, and was wounded at the first battle of Bull Run.

All. Speech! speech! speech!

Estes.   *   *   Government like ours, we have but to—

Jon.   *   *   My name is Jonathan Bunker, [*brings his sword down on the floor,*] and I'm here.

[*Estes shakes his hand, laughingly.*

Estes.   *   *   Want to enlist as a soldier.

Jon.   *   *   Be a sojer agin in two minutes.

Dun. Mr. Bunker, while we admire your patriotism, we fear you are almost too old a man to endure the fatigue of a soldier's life.

Jos. * * So I took down the old critter, [*swings sword around*] and we're here.

Estes. * * Really come down to enlist.

Jon. * * These secesbers is licked anyhow.

Dun. * · * Suppose you postpone the matter till to-morrow.

Jon. * * Then my name aint Jonathan Bunker.

Estes. * * As long as we can.

Jon. * * I don't want you to git 'em mixed.

Estes. * * You are corporal.

Dun. Gentlemen, I propose three cheers for Corporal Bunker, the first volunteer from the village of ——

[*Cheers.*

Jon. * * Come up, fellows, come up,

[*Hale starts and boys follow.*

Hale. Boys, there is not one of you here that has more to see to at home than I have. Remember, I am the only man there; but boys, our country is in danger, and will we stay at home for the few dollars and cents we may save by so doing, and allow the old flag to trampled in the dust by a band of rebels? Not I, *never.* Mother and sister Anna can manage pretty well, and from now on, until this rebellion is crushed they must do the best they can. I follow Jonathan Bunker, and I hope none of you will stand back. [*Hale goes up and signs roll—boys hesitate.*

Estes. * * There will be no hesitency.

[*Boys cheer Hale, and all crowd around to sign.*

Jon. * * We'd been ready for 'em.

Estes. * * I will administer the oath.

[*Drills Squad.*

Estes. Well, boys, hold up your right hands and I will administer the oath.

[*Curtain falls on* Estes *administering the oath.*

SCENE II.

Exterior of JONATHAN BUNKER'S *house—Small stone at* R. *—Door at* C.*—Bench each side—Enter* MARIAR BUNKER C. *door.*

Mariar. 'Pears to me Jonathan ought to got home long

ago. That's the great trouble with him; when he goes to town, he never knows when to come back. I shouldn't wonder if he'd——

Jon. *   *   I'm a reg'lar——

[*Stops on seeing* MARIAR, *and tries to appear sober.*]

Mariar. [*Angrily.*] Jonathan, I'm ashamed of you. I havn't seen you tight before since the Fourth of July.

Jon. *   *   Mrs. Corporal Bunker.

Mariar. Well, that's some excuse, [*pleased*]; for as much as I hate rum, I'd rather see you drunk and true blue, than sober and a traitor, like old Deacon Wise.

Jon. *   *   [*Supports himself against the cottage and comes to a carry.*] And I'm here.

Mariar. [*Angrily.*] Yes, I should say you was here.

Jon. *   *   I'll resign and won't go.

Mariar. Well, when are you going?

Jon. *   *   Goin' to fight. Hooray.

Mariar. Come, Jonathan, let's go in; the neighbors will see you.

Jon. *   *   Hoora for the war! hoora, Mariar, hoora.

Mariar. Come, Jonathan, let's go in.

[*Jonathan starts to go—Returns and looks on the bench, under the bench, and on the ground.*]

Mariar. [*As if afraid he would be seen.*] Come, Jonathan, Come.

Jon. Mariar have you seen may ht?

Mariar. Yes, you old fool; its on your sword.

Jon. *   *   I meant my other hat.

Mariar. Why, you aint got any other one.

[MARIAR *goes and sits on bench at* R. *of door.*

Jon. *   *   Why don't you take it?.

Mariar. Why, I didn't want it. Jonathan.

Jon. *   *   If I'd known that, I wouldn't got off.

Mariar. [*Looking off* L. 1 E.] Come, there comes Squire Dunham.   [*Exit into Cottage.*

Dun. [*Enter* L. 1 E.] Why, Jonathan, you beat me.

Jon. *   *   To see you a little sprung.

Dun. Oh, I guess you are mistaken, Jonathan.

Jon. * * You've been bathing for the rheumatiz.

Dun. [*Going.*] Well, Jonathan, I hope you will come back all right.

Jon. * * I'm gettin' ready now to go off. Good-by Squire. [*Shakes his hand violently, and when he lets go falls on his hands.*]

Dun. Why, Jonathan, you are most too demonstrative, [*going toward him,.* Let me help you.

Jon. Something wrong here. [*Discovers the door way on the other side of the door—Laughs to himself.*]

Mariar. [*From inside, calling.*] Jonathan! Jonathan!

Jon. Hoora for the war! Hoora! [*Enter door.*]

CURTAIN.

ACT III.

SCENE I.

Interior of residence at Rome, Ga.—Sam, a contraband, arranging fire in fireplace R., *with wood, &c., singing.*

Sam. "Massa run, ha! ha!
De darkey stay, ho! ho!
It must be now de Kingdom's comin'.
And de year of jubalo!"

Enter General CORSE C. *door, booted and spurred—The rattling of the saber frightens* SAM *and he falls over the wood.*

De Lord lub you, massa, how you skeered me. I knowed you was a comin', kase some ob de critter company was here, and dey tole de niggers to look sharp; dat Massa Linkum's sogers had gained de day, and de great Captain of de companies he'd be heah; and now you'se come, massa, I hopes you'll make yourself to home. De fire is burnin, and de hoe-cake 's bakin' on de board; supper'll be ready in a minute, and dis yeah chile is de happiest nigger in de Souf.

Corse. That's all right, uncle, but hurry up the supper [*SAM exits, singing,* R 2 E.—CORSE *removing his saber.*

Well, I declare, here are headquarters all arranged, and
a mighty comfortable place too, after a hard day's fight.
[*Throws himself on the sofa.*] None but a poor slave of the
South would have prepared a reception like this for a
Northern soldier. [*Looking around.*] I wonder where the
old reb has gone anyway, that owns this establishment.
[*Knocks at door* L. 2 E.] Come in.

 Estes. [*Enter* L. 2 E., *saluting.*] What orders, General?

 Corse. Are the troops all in camp?

 Estes. Yes, General.

 Corse. Plenty of wood and water?

 Estes. Yes, General.

 Corse. How about forage?

 Estes. Very little, General.

 Corse. How is that? I saw plenty at the white house
with the porch in front, we passed just after the battle.

[Rising.

 Estes.   *   *   Didn't get any there.

 Corse. Why? Who lives there—anybody with a safe-
guard?

 Estes.   *   *   A beautiful face.

 Corse. Ah! I see; and her beauty stands sentinel over
her forage. [*Enter Captain Q. M.* HARKNESS, L. 2 E., *saluting—To* HARKNESS.] Captain, has all the forage been
secured in the neighborhood?

 Hark. Nearly all.

 Corse. That won't do; forage is as necessary as ammunition, and I want my quartermaster to understand no-
body is exempt from furnishing it.

 Hark. Well, sir, I sent Captain Foster to that large
house just outside our lines, but his wagons came back
empty; then I sent Captain Bell, and he failed; finally, I
went myself, and the lady treated us so splendidly, and
talked so sweetly, we really had not the heart to take anything she had.

 Corse. [*Meditatingly.*] Captain, have your wagons
ready at 7 o'clock in the morning. [*To* ESTES.] Order a
strong detail to accompany us. I'll go out with you, Cap-

tain and we'll see about this forage business.

Estes. Will I go with you, General?

Corse. No, sir, I don't want all of my handsome staff-officers with me when I go foraging. [*They laugh—To* HARKNESS.] Attend to your detail Captain, and tell the officers that I will be happy to see them at head-quarters to-night. [*Exit* HARKNESS, L. 2 E.—*Enter* SAM, R. 2 E. *with supper, and arranges it for* CORSE *and* ESTES—*they sit by the table.*] Now, uncle, you appear to be fond of singing, while we eat the hoe-cake, suppose you give us a song.

Sam. All right, massa, all right; but you see I'se dun got to be pretty old, massa, and uncle Sam can't sing de songs like he used to.

Corse. [*Enter officers*, L. 2 E.] Gentlemen, take some supper, you see we are at home here. Uncle Sam runs this plantation now, [*pointing to* SAM,] and I know he's glad to see you; ain't you, uncle?

Sam. Yes, massa; I know'd you was a comin', for de good book said so. De good Lord has heard de prayer meetin's, and de angel ob de Lord hab come down to set de darkeys free. I'se kept de lamps trimmed and burnin' and now, de bridegrooms am come, and may de good Lord bress you all till you dies.

Estes. *   *   Have to go the other way.

Corse. If you wish to test uncle Sam's hoe-cake, gentlemen, sit by.

All. No, thank you, General.

Corse. We've marched and fought now for over a hundred days, but Atlanta has fallen at last, and now we will have a little rest. [*To* ESTES.] What regiment guards the roads and bridges?

Estes. Colonel Atkins with the ninety-second Illinois.

Corse. Then all is safe. Now, uncle, can you favor us with a song?

Sam. If you'll 'scuse de failin's, massa, I'll try.

[SAM *sings* "*Down upon de Swanee River*," *invisible chorus--Bugle-call tattoo in cavalry camp in the distance*

Hark. There goes tattoo in the cavalry camp.

[*All starting up.*]

Estes. [*Offering whisky.*] Will you take a little pizen before you go? [*All fill up and drink—Sing "Rally Round the Flag"—Drum beats tattoo near by, as if from infantry camp—All exit L. 2 E., followed by* ESTES.] Good-night, General.

Corse. [*Lying on the sofa.*] Now for a little rest, undisturbed, 1 hope, by firing on the picket-line—the first quiet twelve hours in one hundred days and nights; but how long will this last? Hood is desperate, and we so far from our base of supplies; nearly two millions rations, ammunition and supplies of all kinds at Allatoona Mountains, defended only by one regiment. Let me see, whose is it? [*Going to table and examining papers—reads.*] Colonel Andrews, Fourth Minnesota, four hundred muskets, and three guns of the Tenth Wisconsin Battery, a small but excellent command; but should Hood interpose between Sherman and me, he could certainly strike that point before I could relieve it, and what a disaster to the whole army —it would be fatal! By to-morrow night my railroad will be completed; I shall place every available man and contraband upon it In the morning and I shall be ready for them. And now for a little sleep. [*Lying down.*] How Allatoona runs in my head—Allatoona. [*Closes his eyes—Tremulo, "Home, Sweet Home"—Shot is heard in the distance—sitting up—another shot is heard.*] Firing on the pickets again. No rest for the soldier. [*Listens and lies down again—a volley is heard in the distance—Springs to his feet.*]

Estes. [*Enter L. 2 E.*] Heavy firing on the picket-line, General.

Corse. Yes, I heard the first shot.

Estes. Shall I arouse the camp?

Corse. No, when we hear from the old Ninety-second 'twill be time enough. Let the men rest. Hark!

[*Horse approaches at L.*

Hale. [*At L. off stage.*] Halt! who comes there?

Horseman. [HARKNESS, *at a distance.*] Friend, with the countersign.

Hale. Dismount, friend. [*Pause and clash of saber.*]
Advance and give the countersign. [*Pause.*] Counter-
sign is correct. Advance.
Hark. Is the General awake?
Hale. I think so.

Enter Captain HARKNESS.

Corse. Well, Captain, what news?
Hark. Colonel Atkins desires me to say, sir, that the
enemy in considerable force have attacked his outlying
pickets, but have been repulsed.
Corse. Were you present, Captain?
Hark. Yes, General.
Corse. Was it cavalry or infantry?
Hark. Cavalry, I think, sir, from the ring of their car-
bines.
Corse. Very well. Tell Colonel Atkins to hold his
front, if possible, without disturbing the command. This
attack is probably to annoy us. [*Exit* HARKNESS.] This
attack tells me Hood is moving and we shall have sharp
work in a few days. [*Exit* ESTES, L. 2 E.—*Sits at table—
Takes papers and map from his pocket.*] Kilpatrick's last
report to Sherman places Hood's advance on Flint River.
That was two days ago, and here are his cavalry now on
my front. Can it be he has crossed the Chattahoochee?
[*Rising.*] He must have done so, if this is not one of
Wheeler's raids. [*Sits at table and examines map.*] Here
is Kenesaw Mountain—here runs the Sweetwater to the
right—Kilpatrick with his cavalry guards the stream—his
pickets should be on the Chattahoochee in front of Hood.
There *we* are twenty miles away; here runs my railroad,
and there is Allatoona with only Kilpatrick's cavalry between it and Hood's whole army. To me this seems very
serious. Allatoona must be a *very* strong place, or Sherman would never have made it his immediate base of supplies. Well, I hope it is, for I have a premonition that I
am to defend it, and that right soon. [*Lying down again.*]
Allatoona! Allatoona! [*Sleeps.*

(*Change.*)

SCENE II.

Morning—Grounds adjoining camp—Reveille is beat—Sentinel, HALE, pacing his beat—Enter JONATHAN BUNKER, L. 1 E., with his shoulder hanging full of chickens and other articles of food. .

Hale. Halloo, Jonathan, you're out early.

Jon. *   * Swearin' in poultry.

Hale. Pretty good luck, eh?

Jon. *   * I had to take him to the guard-house anyway. Any news?

Hale. Nothing particular, I guess. They say we're going to do big things pretty soon, as usual.

Jon. *   * Sent what was left of him home in a letter.

Hale. They'll probably change the theatre of war to Georgia.

Jon. *   * I guess I'll git. [*Exit* R 1 E.

Enter HARKNESS *and* WAGONMASTER, L. 1 E.

Hark. Is your train all ready?

W. Master. Yes, Captain, all ready.

Hark. Is the detail a strong one?

W. Master. Yes, sir, Colonel Estes goes in command.

Hark. We go outside the lines, and the enemy may be nearer than we suspect. There was firing on the picket line last night. At seven o'clock move out on the road toward Burnt Hickory, and we will overtake you with the escort. This way. [*Exit* L. 2 E.

(*Change.*)

SCENE III. ˙

Interior of a room at Woodlawn Plantation—LOTTIE and HOWE at R.—MAY FULLER and Major (Doctor) GRAVES at R. in conversation.

Howe. Lottie, I know not how to advise you; this terrible defeat of Hood leaves our State almost entirely unprotected, and if Sherman's army should pass this way,

I shall be obliged to leave you, I know not for how long.

Lottie. No matter, brother; I am a Southern woman, and know my duty.

Howe. Ah! Lottie, you don't know the character of those Northern vandals; the torch would be applied before you could—— [*Bugle-call heard outside.*

Lottie. Hark! what is that? [*All rush to window.*

Enter REBEL SOLDIER C. *door.*

Soldier. Fly! fly for your lives; the Yankees are close upon us.

Graves. Where are they?

Sol. Not half a mile away.

Howe. Tell Colonel Hubbel to attack them and hold them in check; I'll come to his support immediately with the reserve. [*Exit* SOLDIER C. *door.*] Good-by, Lottie; Good-by, May. Remember you are Southern women, and give these Yankees the reception they deserve.

Lottie. Have no fears, brother, have no fears.

May. Depend on us. [*Shouts heard outside.*

Howe. [*Rushes to* C. *door.*] By heavens! the house is surrounded and my men are flying. Curse the cowards; we'll be captured sure.

Lottie. No! no! [*Opens door at* R.] Go in here; they shall not take you. [HOWE *and* GRAVES *enter the room—* HOWE *drops a glove—To* MAY.] Now, May, our courage is to be put to the severest test. His life depends on us; as you love him, so be brave.

May. Oh! I will try; I will do my best.

[*Enter* CORSE C. *door, with drawn saber, followed by* HARKNESS.]

Corse. [*Starting back.*] I beg pardon, ladies; I expected to find armed men here, not ladies.

Lottie. I only wish we were men, you would not enter this house so easily.

May. And so do I. [MAY *and* HARKNESS *go up stage.*

Corse. [*Sheathing his sword.*] And I prefer you to remain the same beautiful ladies you were created. I never could resist an army of soldiers with such eyes as yours.

But, ladies, were there no others here before we entered?

Lottie. Do you suppose a Southern gentleman would remain housed, when the enemy's bugle summoned him to battle?

Corse. Well, that depends on the man more than the section or locality he comes from. But no matter; if concealed, he cannot escape, for my men surround the house.

Lottie. [*Haughtily.*] We are prisoners then, I suppose; or do you come to fire the house? I believe that is a favorite pastime with you Yankee soldiers.

Corse. No, no, ladies, neither; your sex and your home shall be respected. We do not come to make war on women; but you have a large amount of forage, my men and animals need it, and I have come to take it.

Lottie. Indeed; may I ask your name?

Corse. Certainly, my dear madam, my name is Corse.

Lottie. General Corse?

Corse. Yes, madam.

Lottie. Are Yankee Generals so much better thieves than their quartermaster, that they go foraging themselves.

Corse. Well, no, madam; my quartermasters have no fears of rebel bullets or rebel shells, but your fascinations have driven them from the field, and they report to me as incapable of making even the second attack; I am therefore obliged to go myself.

Lottie. This attempt at flattery may be very amusing to you, but it is very distasteful to me. I ask no favor, sir, and expect none. Take all I have, sir, take it all; sooner or later it must all go, and I am powerless to prevent you.

Corse. Madam, you are not powerless, and while I denounce my quartermasters for their weakness, I plead guilty myself, nor do I say this for flattery. [*To* HARKNESS.] Captain, take that only which our immediate necessities require. See that no depredations are committed, and let this disagreeable duty be over as soon as possible. [*Exit* HARKNESS, C. *door.*

Lottie. I am sure I thank you. and I now beg pardon for my unkind words spoken a few moments ago. Will you be seated?

Corse. Thank you. [*Going toward the door as if to sit, discovers a gauntlet on the floor—picks it up.*] What is this, ladies?

Lottie. [*Confused.*] A glove. I think.

Corse. Does it belong to either of you?

Both. [*Confused.*] No, sir.

Corse. [*Sharply.*] Certainly not; this is a soldier's gauntlet: to whom does it belong?

Lottie. There was a soldier here just before you came, but he left us, sir.

Corse. [*As if unsatisfied.*] Very well; I'll not distress you.

May. [*To* LOTTIE.] We must do something or we are lost.

Corse. [*Interrupting.*] I beg pardon, ladies.

Lottie. Nothing sir; my friend thought perhaps you would take some refreshments. Will you take a glass of wine?

Corse. [*Aside.*] She is charming indeed. I think I will. [*To* LOTTIE.] Oh, yes, with pleasure. [*Sitting.*] I don't wonder, madam, my officers failed to take your corn and hay.

Lottie. And why, pray?

Corse. Why I am more than half inclined to order the wagons to unload.

[*Enter* MAY, R. *door, with cake and wine.*

May. Will you have some wine, sir?

Corse. [*To* LOTTIE.] Will you join me?

Lottie. Oh, yes; and it is not the first Yankee I have drank wine with, either.   [*They all drink.*

Corse. Well, ladies, [*rising,*] I shall be obliged to bid you good morning; and rest assured, I shall never forget this happy meeting.

Lottie. General, do you love music.

Corse. Oh, yes; but it is a long time since I've heard a lady sing.

Lottie. [*Going to piano.*] What shall I sing?

Corse. Oh? anything: even a rebel song would sound sweetly, no doubt, if sung by you.

[LOTTIE *sings "Bonnie Blue Flag.*

Lottie. You see I am a true rebel.

Corse. I could forgive all the rebels if they were as charming as you.

Lottie. Now, that compliment deserves something better than a rebel song. I used to sing a song long years ago, before this war had made us enemies; I learned it at West Point, [*sitting at piano*], and I will sing it for you. [*Sings "Bennie Havens Oh"—while she is singing,* ESTES *enters at* C. *door and approaches her slowly as if recognizing her voice, and joins in the chorus—*LOTTIE *falters and stops, finally starts up from the piano before the song is concluded —turns to* ESTES.] Estes! why my old friend, Cadet Estes!

Corse. [*Whistles.*] Why, what is this?

Estes. *   *   Have you no word of welcome?

Lottie. Welcome! why, what welcome can I give to you? Would you have me welcome to this house a man who comes to take my brother's life, and rob his defenceless family? Welcome such a man? If you respect me, sir, how can you ask me such a question.

Estes. *   *   As it possibly can be to you.

[*Shots are heard outside at* L.—*Bugle sounds the assembly.*]

Corse. There goes the assembly! We are attacked! [*More shots heard—Bugle sounds quick time.*] Farewell, ladies, till we meet again.   [*Exit* C. *door.*

Estes. *   *   Say that I may return!

Lottie. [*Aside.*] Oh! what can I say! [*More shots heard.*] You will be killed if you stay. Yes, yes, you may come, but go now.

Estes. *   *   Die in the attempt. Farewell!

[*Exit* C. *door.*

HOWE *and* MAJOR *rush into room, and all crowd to the window at* L.

Howe. Stand back. [*Draws his pistol and throws open the window.*] There goes my enemy, and I have sworn to kill him. Harry Estes, 'tis my turn now. [*Presents the pistol—*LOTTIE *throws up her hand, and it is discharged into the air.*] Curse you, I've missed him; but it's not yet too late.

[*Leaps out of the window—*LOTTIE *falls on the sofa and covers her face with her hands—clashing of sabres outside and some firing.*]

May. [*Looking from the window.*] Oh? he will be killed! He has mounted his horse, and there he goes into the midst of the fight! [*Starting back.*] Oh! they're fighting!

Lottie. [*Going to the window and taking* MAY'S *hand.*] He has fallen—he has killed my brother. O my God! [*Falls upon the sofa—*MAY *goes to her.*] Go see what they have done with him.

May. [*Goes to the window.*] The Yankees have gone and they are bringing Charley toward the house.

[LOTTIE *rises, and they arrange the sofa for him—Enter* HOWE *with a sabre-cut on the head, assisted by* GRAVES.]

Lottie. O Charley! are you badly wounded?

Howe. Yes. [*They place him on the sofa.*] Curse that Yankee lover of yours; I trusted to my revolver and missed him, and then he sabred me. [MAY *brings bandages, and Major binds up his head.*] This is the second time he has triumphed over me; but by heavens, if we meet again, he shall die.

Graves. It's a bad wound, Charley; that Lincoln hireling struck to kill, but you will be all right in a week.

Howe. Lottie, I must leave you; it will be impossible for me to remain here; 'tis too near the Yankee lines.

Lottie. O brother! you can stay at least til you are better.

Howe. [*Angrily.*] Yes, to be captured by that Yankee lover of yours. How nice that would be!

Lottie. [*Angrily.*] Brother!

Howe. Oh! you can't deceive me; I saw your meeting. You must take me for a fool. You love this fellow.

Lottie. [*Firmly.*] Well, what if I do?

Howe. What if you do? Do you hear that, Major? She confesses it. Oh shame! shame upon you—a Southern woman, a Howe, and love an accursed Yankee!

Graves. Come, Colonel, we must go; these Yankees may return.

Howe. Well, I suppose we must. [*Rising.*] But I tell you, Major, it's hard to be driven from one's home, to leave the old homestead that has sheltered one from childhood. If I thought the Yankees would push their lines beyond this house and occupy it, I'd burn it to the ground. But come, Lottie, let us have some refreshments before we go; it may be the last I shall ever taste under the old roof.

Lottie. We'll bring it, brother.

Howe. Well, I reckon you will have to, for I expect the damned niggers have all run away. [*Exit* LOTTIE *and* MAY R. 2 E.] Major, the man who struck me down, you remember him? It was Harry Estes, a classmate of ours at West Point. Our enmity is of long standing. Through his means I was dismissed the service, and I vowed that if I ever met him, I would take his life. He has been successful to-day, and but for him, we would have captured the whole of the Yankee forces.

Graves. That is so, Colonel; but give the devil his due: he's a splendid soldier. The daring manner in which he dashed among his men, rallied them, and held us back until his wagons got away, was really beautiful. That's when he struck you, Colonel.

Howe. Yes, I know it. [*Hesitating.*] Major, I've a plan to capture him yet.

Graves. How?

Howe. Send May to me and keep Lottie away for a time and you shall see.

Graves. All right.   [*Exit* R. 1 E.

Howe. So, so; there no way one-half so easy to catch a man as to bait your hook with a woman; and when Harry Estes shall become my prisoner, I'll invent a hundred ways to humiliate him. [*Looking around, in a low tone.*] If he should happen to shoot himself accidentally, of course, that wouldn't be my fault. It's a long lane that has no turn, and I'll be even with him yet. A little patience.

May, [*Enter* R. 2 E.] The Major says you desire to speak with me.

Howe. Yes; come here, May. [*She sits by his side.*] Do you love the Southern cause.

May. [*Surprised.*] How can you ask me such a question?

Howe. Because a woman's heart is to me strangely incomprehensible. Yesterday—this morning, I would have risked the fate of the Southern Confederacy and staked my life on my sister's loyalty.

May. Would you now hesitate.

Howe. Yes; I would not be unjust, but from this time forth, she must know nothing which, if imparted to the enemy, would injure our cause. But you, May, you can be trusted.

May. I am a weak, timid woman, but I love the South— I love you, Charley, and I would die to save either.

Howe. I rejoice to hear you say so. I believe you, and know *you* can be trusted. But, dear girl, I will not ask so great a sacrifice, though I am to ask of you a service full of importance to me and to our cause.

May. [*Surprised.*] Of me, Charlie? Why, what can I do.

Howe. Much—everything. May, you know this Yankee lover of Lottie's?

May. Yes, I knew him at West Point.

Howe. You have heard of his exploits, and the injuries he and his chief, General Corse, have inflicted on our people?

May. Yes, the negroes are continually talking about them.

Howe. They must be captured, and 'tis in your power to do it.

May. [*Surprised.*] What!—I Charley?

Howe. Yes, you. Now listen. When we have gone, suggest to Lottie that she shall invite him over here to dine——

May. Oh! she would never do that.

Howe. [*Taking her hand.*] Then you do it. Stop. I'll tell you what's better. Write a letter to General Corse, in her name, stating you wish to see him in regard to protecting property—anything.

May. But suppose——

Howe. Never fear, he will come—Estes sure; then inform me; with a strong force I will dash down upon the house, kill or disperse his escort, and their capture is certain.

May. O Charley! Lottie would hate me forever.

Howe. What! do you refuse?

[*Casts away her and.*

May. No, no, Charley; this would be so dishonorable, so treacherous.

Howe. [*Rising.*] May, any stratagem is fair in war, and we are justified in using any means to crush an enemy like that with which we are contending. Step by step we have been driven back from the borders, till now we have reached the very heart of Georgia. For a whole month you have seen the sad spectacle of roads filled with helpless people; old age and infancy, hand in hand, fleeing before these ruthless invaders; for weeks you have seen the heavens grow black with smoke ascending from Southern homes now lain in ashes. Their sabres have grown red with the blood of those who would defend their hearthstones against overwhelming odds, and you with your own eyes, not an hour since saw me struck down by this accursed Yankee; you heard the dying groans of our people as his minions trampled them in the dust, and yet you will not raise a finger against such a foe.

May. Say no more. To prove my devotion, I'll do it. I'll do all you ask—even more.

Howe. [*Takes her hand.*] Hush, darling, here they come; remember, not a word to Lottie. Send your letter through the Yankee picket-lines and leave the rest to me. Hush!

Lottie. [*Enter* R. 2 E.] Lunch is ready, gentlemen.

What, alone? Where is the Major!
Honce. He'll be here in a moment. [*Enter* MAJOR.
Lottie. Come, Major, lunch is ready.
Howe. May and I will follow in a moment. |*Exit* LOT-
TIE *and* MAJOR R. 2. E.] Now, May, remember—not a
word to Lottie, not a word.
May. Not one word, Charley.
  [*Jim, a contraband, separates curtains hanging in front
  of an alcove from behind, and sticks his head through
  the opening—Exit* HOWE *and* MAY R. 2 E.]
Jim. Oh! no, not a word to anybody, Massa—oh! no,
not a word.
                    CURTAIN.

                   ACT IV.
                   SCENE I.

General CORSE'S *head-quarters at Rome, Ga.—Same as Act
III, Scene I.—*CORSE *and* ESTES *sitting at Table* R.—
CORSE *reading morning reports.*

Estes. *   *   We are to be left behind.
Corse. No, sir; when old Tecumseh moves, we move
with him. Walcott's brigade is the only command save
ours armed with Spencers—that is, of the infantry. I believe all of Kilpatrick's men have Spencers.
Officer. [*At* L. 2 E.] Detail halt! order arms! rest!

Enter Capt. HARKNESS *and Major* ANDREWS, *old and new
          officer of the day.*

Corse. Well, Major, what news from the front?
Andrews. All quiet; yet I would recommend a strong
force on the Burnt Hickory road, for since the attack on
the foraging party yesterday, the enemy have been seen
frequently on our front. Here is a letter sent to the outlying pickets this morning.   [*Gives letter to* CORSE.
Corse. [*To* HARKNESS.] You go out, sir, with the relief.
Hark. Yes, General.
Corse. Well, look sharp; to-morrow I'll increase the

force under your command. [*Exit* HARKNESS *and* AN-
DREWS L. 2 E.—*Opens the letter.*] Halloo! what's this? A
letter from a woman! Guess it must be for you, Estes.

Estes. Let me see.

Corse. No, I'll read it first. [*Reads.*]

"GENERAL CORSE; GENERAL: The unfortunate occur-
rence at my house yesterdaay, and the precarious position in which two helpless women find themselves at this
trying hour, induces me to ask of you some protection and
assistance. Perhaps it would be best for us to abandon
our home and go further South, beyond the dangers that
now threaten us. Will you honor us with another visit,
that I may consult with you in regard to what we had
better do? I blush to ask a favor of an enemy, but my
own people are powerless to aid us.

"Yours, LOTTIE HOWE."

"P. S.—I trust you and Colonel Estes were not injured
yesterday, and may I ask that he will accompany you."

Yes, yes, of course—move South—precarious position—
two helpless females—yes, yes—hope Colonel Estes will
come too—[*Writes on the back of the letter and reads.*]
"Respectfully referred to Colonel Estes."

[*Gives him the letter.*

Estes. [*Seriously.*] General!

Corse. Oh! that's all right, Colonel; don't take offense.
Go and see the girl.

Estes. Will you go, General?

Corse. No, why should I go? That letter was really
intended for you. [*Laughing.*] Go and see her, go and
see her. Two poor helpless females. [*Laughs.*] But
have a care, Estes, it's near the rebel lines, and fair as
she is, she may be treacherous.

Estes. No, General; treacherous?—never!

Corse. But remember, I've warned you. I'm going up
the railroad.   *Exit* CORSE L. 2 E.

*Estes * * Sergeant! sergeant!

Jonathan. [*Enter* L. 2 E.] I'm here.

Estes. * * Take charge of the office.

[*Exit* L. 2 E.

Jon. * * If they do, I'm goin' to Congress

Enter Orderly HALE, L. 2 E.—*Keeps his hat on.*

Hale. Where's the General?

Jon. * * Take your hat off when you talk to me.

Hale. Oh! what's the matter, Jonathan? Are you drunk?

Jon. * * My grandfather fit and died in the Revolution, and——

Hale. Look here, Jonathan, I ain't got no time to fool; there's a darkey outside, and says he must see the General. [JONATHAN *looks at him very dignified*—HALE *takes off his hat and salutes.*] Ain't you going to treat, General?

Jonathan. * * Nothing like being an officer and having command.

Hale. Well, General [*Puts on his hat.*] what about——

Jonathan. [*Angrily.*] Take off your hat, sir!

Hale. [*Takes off his hat hastily.*] Well, General, what about the nigger?

Jonathan. * * I want my mind clear.

Hale. [*Saluting very humbly and going towards the whiskey.*] When will we move, General? [*Ventures to take a glass of whiskey.*] Here's hoping you'll be a Major General in six weeks. [*Drinks.*]

Jonathan. All right.

[*Struggle is heard outside at* L. 2 E. *Enter Jim, arranging his clothes as if they had been pulled and goes toward* HALE.]

Jim. [*To* HALE.] Is you de Captin, Massa?

Jonathan. [*Indignantly.*] Don't you see I'm here, nigger? What do you want?

Jim. Massa, whar is de Gineral dat had de fight yesterday ober at Massa Howe's plantation?

Jonathan. Well, he aint here. What do you want?

Jim. [*Alarmed.*] Is dey gone already, Massa?

Jonathan. Gone where?

Jim. Ober to de plantation, if dey has dey'll perish. Dey's betrayed, Massa, dey's betrayed.

Jonathan. What do you mean, you black rascal?

Jim. Massa, I dunno, I dunno zackly, but dey'll boff be killed if dey's gone. For de lub ob de Lord send somebody to bring dem back. 'Tis all a trick and Massa Howe is waitin' wit his sogers ober dar to cotch 'em.

Jon. * * Where is Sam? [*Calling.*] Sam! Sam! [*to Hale.*] Where's Corse?

Hale. Sam said he went up the railroad.

Jon. * * When I'm in command.

Jim. No, Massa, as I hope to lib I've told de troof, and somebody will be sorry for all dis.

Jon. [*Indignant.*] What's that? Nigger, did you ever see the inside of a guard-house?

Jim. No, Massa.

Jon. * * Take him to the guard house.

[*Exit* HALE *with* JIM *in charge,* L. 2 E.]

Jim. May de Lord protect 'em. Ise done my best.

[*Enter* HALE L 2 E., *hat on.*

Hale. [*Laughing.*] Jonathan, you ought to seen——

Jon. * * My grandfather fit and died and——

[*Enter* CORSE L. 2 E. JONATHAN *removes his hat and comes down out of the General's chair very humbly.*

Corse. Where is Colonel Estes?

Jon. * * Back in an hour or two.

Corse. [*Carelessly.*] Oh yes, I know. Any one been yere since I left? [*Looking at whiskey.*

Jon. * * I put him in the guard-house.

Corse. Why, what for?

Jon. * * And you would be took.

Corse. What! What's that you say? Where is the negro? Bring him here instantly. [*Exit* JONATHAN *and* HALE, L. 2 E.] What can this mean? By heavens! I fear some treachery. I didn't think he would go before I got back. [*Pacing the floor.* Why don't they come? [*Enter* JONATHAN *and* HALE *with* JIM L. 2 E.] Uncle, what is this story I hear?

Jim. [*Taking his hand.*] Is you here, Massa! De Lord be bressed! Had you gone ober to de plantation dey would killed you suah, case I heerd dem make de plan wid Massa Howe.

Corse. Is this true, Uncle?

Jim. Yes, Massa.

Corse. [*To* JONATHAN.] Jonathan, Colonel Estes will

be killed or captured through your stupidity. Quick! no
time is to be lost! Order out the escort! Sound boots and
saddles! [*Exit* JONATHAN L. 2 E.] [*To* HALE.] Orderly,
saddle the black mare—see that my revolvers are ready—
quick.
  [*Exit* HALE L. 2 E.—*boots and saddles is sounded outside.* *Exit* CORSE L. 2 E.]
  (*Change.*)

SCENE II.

Grove near Woodlawn.—Enter HOWE *and* GRAVES.

Howe. [*Putting on his gloves.*] Major, it's all right; we
have not waited in vain; our plan works well, for May has
informed me the Yankees have bit at my bait. It's near
nine o'clock. Be ready, men, I will [*speaking from wing at
R.*] give the signal; then dash down upon them. [*Pleased.*]
ha! ha!

Graves. Howe, this manner of warfare is not honorable:
you yourself would denounce it if adopted by the Yankees
themselves.

Howe. Do you suppose I will leave any means unem-
ployed to capture that fellow?

Graves. Any means, Colonel?

Howe. [*Emphatically.*] Yes, any.

Graves. Well, if you have resolved, have you consider-
ed what the result may be if you fail?

Howe. But I shall not fail.

Graves. Don't be too sure, Colonel, don't be too sure.
These Yankees are aware of the risk to which they are
exposed—they're no fools.

Howe. [*Recklessly.*] Well, we'll try it any way.

Graves. Of course, you are the commanding officer and
can do just as you may choose, but mark my word, if you
fail and this trick is discovered, your home will be burnt
to the ground, and May and Lottie will be obliged to go to
the Yankee General for protection, and you yourself may
lose your life.

Howe. Do you suppose you can frighten me from my

purpose? I tell you the prize is within my reach and I have but to grasp it. If *you* are afraid you are excused from going.

Graves. Colonel, my duties as a surgeon lead me where my services are required—'tis not for me to approve or disapprove; but to save the lives of those who may be stricken down, I shall go; but the consequences shall rest entirely on yourself.

Howe. Well, let it sir. I do not wish to shirk the responsibility.

[*Enter Rebel Sergeant* R. 2 E.]

Sergeant. Half a dozen Yankees have just rode up toward your house, sir.

Howe. All right, they've come; now be ready.

Sergeant. Shall we kill them?

Howe. Kill the men if you are obliged to, but take the officers prisoners. I *want* them. Where are the men?

Sergeant. They are concealed, sir, in the grove.

Howe. Now, gentlemen, if you want to see me bag a Yankee General and his adjutant follow me.

[*Exit all* R. 2 E.]

[*Change.*]

SCENE III.

[*Interior at Woodlawn—same as Act III, Scene III—*LOT-TIE *seated at table* R., MAY *looking out of window at* L.

Lottie. May, you have been standing at that window for the past hour. Whom are you expecting? Have you any idea Charley will visit us again?

May. [*Confused.*] Oh! no, Lottie, I'm a little nervous, that's all.

Lottie. Why, what's the matter?

May. [*Both coming to the front.*] Well, I've been thinking all day of the battle yesterday, and I tremble lest it should be repeated. Your friend is sure to return. Your brother will watch the house, and if he comes——

Lottie. Do you think he will be so foolish?

May. [*Forgetting herself.*] I know he will.

Lottie. [*Excited and surprised.*] You know?

May. [*Checking herself.*] That is—well—why shouldn't he?

Lottie. [*Looking at May surprised.*] Oh! I hope he will not be so rash.

May. [*Going to the window.*] Here comes some horsemen now.

Lottie. [*Alarmed.*] Where? which way? [*Going to the window.*] It is *he*—it is Estes. Oh! why has *he* come here? [*To May.*] What *shall* we do?

May. Receive him—do the best we can.

Estes. * * You see, Miss Lottie, I have returned.

Lottie. [*In fear.*] Oh! why have you been so very reckless—why take such pains to be captured, perhaps killed?

Estes. * * Any foe would prevent me?

Lottie. [*Surprised.*] I bade you come! I never invited you.

Estes. What? Read that. [*Hands her a letter.*]

Lottie. [*Taking it.*] I never wrote it. Harry, you are betrayed, and May, this is your work. Speak! have you done this?

May. [*Confused.*] Yes, oh! yes——

Enter Orderly HALE, C *door.*]

Hale. Colonel, we are surrounded—we have but six men; what shall we do?

Estes. * * Bolt the door.

[HALE *bolts the door—few shots are heard and* HOWE'S *men are heard attempting to force the* door—ESTES *places his pistols on the table in front of him and throws his scabbard one side—*HALE *goes by his side.*]

Howe. [*Outside.*] Open the door and surrender.

Estes. * * They will be here in ten minutes.

Howe. Break down the door!

Lottie. Oh! Harry, you will be killed. What can we do?
[*Door gives way.*]

Estes. Stand aside and let them come. Now Orderly.
[*Firing by all—two rebels fall by the door—*HALE *falls near* ESTES—*Rebels give back.*

Howe. Forward! Come on you cowards. [*Enter* HOWE c *door with drawn sabre, followed by* GRAVES.] [*Clash of sabres outside. Enter* JONATHAN *and two or three men.* JONATHAN *grabs* HOWE *and throws him back.*]

Jon. No you don't. My name's Jonathan Bunker and we're here.

Estes. * * I ask no advantage.

[JONATHAN *goes over to* GRAVES *and stands by him.* ESTES *and* HOWE *cross swords, and* LOTTIE *steps between them.*

Lottie. Spare him, Harry, he is my brother.

Estes. * * Thank your sister for it.

Howe. Strike, sir; I scorn to seek the protection of a woman and I ask no quarter.

[*Enter* CORSE *and* JIM. JONATHAN *and others remove dead soldiers.*]

Corse. Colonel, you are saved and I am glad we arrived in time; but you owe your life to this faithful negro.

Howe. Curse the infernal nigger.

Jim. Cuss away, Massa, cuss away; but it won't do no good, Massa.

[*Enter* JONATHAN *with paper.*]

Jon. * * Amount to something to you.

Corse. [*Takes papers and reads.*] Well! these are indeed valuable. [*Reads aloud.*]

To COLONEL HOWE: Hood's army have crossed the Chattahoochee. Join Hood in front of Allatoona. Hood is advancing on the Sweetwater, driving Kilpatrick's cavalry before him; to-morrow he will reach Allatoona. Don't fail to join him at once.

FRENCH, Major Gen. C. S. A.

[*To* ESTES.] Estes, telegraph immediately to——

Estes. Our telegraph has been useless for two hours.

Corse. Then mount your fleetest horse. It's twenty-five miles from here to Sherman's headquarters. Take a few men, pass to the left of the Sweetwater, skirt the base of Kenesaw mountain (you know the road), then ride for your life. Tell Sherman I am ready and await his orders. If I do not get a telegram from him in less than three hours I shall move without orders. By morning Hood will be in front of Allatoona and then it will be too late. [*To* JONATHAN.] Remove your prisoner, Sergeant. [JONATHAN *exit with prisoners.*] [*To ladies.*] Collect such things as you may need and allow me to escort you to my headquarters, where I shall offer you every protection.

Lottie. Thanks, General. My brother's acts of treachery have left me without a protector.

Estes. *   * Can you—will you trust me?

Lottie. [*Taking his hand hesitatingly.*] Harry, I will.

Corse. Estes, leave this for some other time. Hood is marching on Allatoona. Away! away!

Estes. [*To Lottie.*] I'll meet you at headquarters; farewell, Lottie. [*Kisses her and exits* L. 2 E. *hurriedly.*]

Corse. Now, ladies, we must go.

Lottie. [*With her hands raised toward heaven, looks up imploringly.*] My home! my home! [Picture. Red fire.]
[*Change.*]

SCENE 4.

Landscape in 1—*Some firing and cheering heard outside at* R. *Enter* ESTES *at* R. *fires two or three shots—Two or three rebels enter at* R. *and seize him.*—ESTES *fights desperately but is overpowered.*

Rebel Sergeant. No you don't. We want you. Colonel Howe told me to watch for just such chaps as you. Where was you going, Yank?

Estes. *   * Decline to answer any questions.

Sergeant. Well, we will see about that. Men, you will take this man down to camp. Guard, fall in, right face. [*Sergeant places* ESTES *in the ranks.*] Now, sir, move on, and if you attempt to escape I would not give much for your Yankee skin. Guard, forward march. [*They exit at* L. 1 E.]
[*Change.*]

SCENE 5.

Camp in the woods—Rebel soldiers seated around stage—Enter JIM *with basket of pies and cakes.*

Jim. How are you boys. Do you want to buy some provisions?

Rebel soldier. Now, boys, here's some fun. [*To* Jim.] What have you got in your basket, nigger? [*Fumbles in* Jim's *basket.*]

Jim. Say, you jest keep your dirty fingers out of dem pies. If you want to buy any of 'em, I'm here to wait on yo'.

Soldier. What's that you say, you black rascal? Boys get that blanket and we'll show him how to talk to white folks. [*They get blanket and toss* Jim *up several times.* Jim *finally rolls out of blanket making great fuss.*]

Jim. Say, boy's, dat's usin' a feller mighty rough, I tell you. I don't like dat kind of business no how. [*Aside.*] If Massa Estes gets by this camp he's all right. I done thought I'd watch 'em a little any way.

[*Enter Rebel squad with* ESTES.]

Sergeant. Halt, order arms, break ranks, march. Now, then, men, keep a good watch of him; if he attempts to escape, shoot him. [*Exit* R. 2 E.]

Jim. Bress de Lord if dat aint Massa Estes now. He's gone up now for suah. [*Crosses over to Estes who stands at* R. 2 E.]

Estes. * * Send some one to my relief, Be quick, go.

Jim. Alll right, Massa, Ise gone. [*Exit* R. 2 E. *in haste.*]

[*Enter Sergeant and Rebel Capt.* COOKE, R. 2 E.]

Sergeant. Captain, here is a Yankee Colonel we captured and he says he will answer no questions.

Capt. Cook. All right. Sergeant, we will see about that. [*To Estes.*] Who are you, and where are you from?

Estes. * * Officer from the federal army.

Cooke. Indeed. Be careful, sir, how you answer, or you will be mustered out of the service sooner than you expected. What was your mission so far outside of your lines?

Estes. * * Dare you to injure me you cowardly rebel traitor.

Cook. What's that? Fall in, men, the Yanks are pretty thick around here and the sooner we get rid of this fellow the better. [*Guards fall in.*] [*To* ESTES.] Now, then, will you answer my questions?

Estes. * * I will keep my oath though I lose my life.

Cooke. Then, sir, you have sealed your own doom. Guard, ready, aim,—now, then, if you have anything to say, you had better be quick about it, for your time is short.

Estes. * * And that is [*looks off at* L., *rises up and swings his hat*] surrender!

[JONATHAN *and* JIM *enter at* R. *with squad of Union soldiers—*COOK *falls on floor—*JIM *stands over him triumphantly—Rebels fall on their knees—*JONATHAN *and men stand charge—picture, red fire.*

[CURTAIN.]

ACT V.

SCENE I.

SHERMAN'S *headquarters at Allatoona—*SHERMAN *seated at table* R. *with his adjutant reading dispatches.*

Sherman. Have you any word from Corse?

Col. Foster. No, General, but here is a dispatch from General Kilpatrick.

Sherman. What does he report?

Foster. [*Reads:*]

HEADQUARTERS CAVALRY CORPS,}
10 A. M.{

GENERAL:—This morning the enemy appeared in force on the left bank of the Chattahoochee, drove in my pickets and crossed the river in flat-boats. He is now throwing a pontoon. My entire command is moving to attack him. Respectfully, KILPATRICK.

[*Enter Orderly* R. 1 E.]

Orderly. An officer has just arrived from General Corse.

Sherman. [*Excited.*] From Corse? Show him in. [*Exit Orderly* R. 1 E. *Enter* ESTES R. 1 E. SHERMAN *rises and shakes his hand.*] Why, Colonel, what brings you here?

Estes.   *   *   And is marching for Allatoona.

Sherman. How know you this?

Estes.   *   *   On his person were found these papers. [*Hands letter to* SHERMAN. SHERMAN *takes papers and reads.*]

Sherman. Allatoona was Hood's objective point.

Estes.   *   *   Sent to my relief by General Corse.

Sherman. You have done nobly. Take a fresh horse, gather up all the mounted men here at headquarters and ride to Allatoona and join General Corse. Tell him the whole army will march at once to his relief. [*Exit* ESTES L. 2 E. *Sits at table and writes rapidly.*] This is very serious. [*Enter* FOSTER L. 1 E. *Handing paper to* FOSTER.] There, send that to Howard. [*Exit* FOSTER L. 1 E.] [*Examines map on table; while examining enter* FOSTER. L. 1 E.] Colonel, send Captain Seymour to General Slocum and say I wish to see him immediately. [*Exit* FOSTER L. 1 E.] [*Pacing the floor.*] Hood's ultimate objective point is a mystery to me. I don't believe he even knows himself. I expected some dash on his part, but I had no idea he would be so bold as to attack me in the rear. But I'll make him repent this. [*Enter* SLOCUM L. 1 E.] Slocum, Hood is on this side of the Chattahoochee and is now marching on Allatoona—so report Corse and Kilpatrick. Kilpatrick is fighting him now. It may be he is only moving with part of his command. Howard moves in half an hour and I leave you here for fear of a feint. Use your own judgment, but you had better send a strong force down the river with orders to attack fiercely any force they may meet; it will have a tendency to check Hood's advance. I leave at once for Kenesaw Mountain; I pitch my tents there to-night. Look out for my signals by red light. I placed Corse at Rome in anticipation of this movement. If any officer in my command can hold Allatoona he will do it; so long as he lives Allatoona is safe.

Slocum. I have no doubt of it; he is bravery itself.

[*Enter* FOSTER L. 2 E.] [*To* FOSTER.] Break up headquarters. Sound boots and saddles. In twenty minutes we must be off. [*Exit* FOSTER L. 2 E. *Boots and saddles sounded at* L. *Cheers, etc.*]

Slocum. What splendid soldiers! hear them cheer; always ready for a fight.

Sherman. Well, good bye, Slocum. Hood must be crazy to think he can outflank us old flankers. Good bye. Look out for me on Kenesaw to-night. [*Exit all* L. 1 E.]

(*Change.*)

SCENE II.

Allatoona—Kenesaw Mountain in the distance—Picks and Shovels heard off stage at L.—*A small elevation at* R. *and a signal officer* (BELL) *looking towards Kenesaw and then down as if looking down the side of Allatoona Mountain—Soldiers with muskets etc. on the stage. Colonel* AN-DREWS *heard off stage at* L.]

Andrews. That's right, men—work for your lives. The enemy is only a few miles away, but if he fails to attack us for an hour we are safe. Corse left Rome an hour ago, and will soon be here. [*Enter* L. 1 E.]

Bell. Colonel, will you step here a moment? I see an officer and some men riding furiously along the base of Kenesaw.

Andrews. Who can they be? [*Going on the elevation.*]

Bell. Some one, I think, from Sherman. I can only see them with my glass.

Andrews. Keep watch of them.

[*Enter Capt.* LYKE *of artillery.*]

Lyke. Colonel, do you see that rebel flag?

Andrews. Where?

Lyke. [*Pointing down.*] Down there by that clump of trees.

Andrews. Oh, yes, they've a battery.

Lyke. Yes, they are just coming into position. Let me give them one shot.

Andrews. All right, give it to 'em. [*Exit* LYKE L. *A shot is heard, followed by an explosion in the distance. Men rush up and look off at* R. *They cheer.*] Bully for Lyke! There goes a caisson!

Bell. There is another rebel flag. Yes, and there is another. [*Pointing.*]

Andrews. And here are more on our right—rebels everywhere. Oh! why don't Corse come? Can they have captured him? Men, prepare for——

[*Enter* JONATHAN L. 2 E. *in haste.*]

Jonathan. I'm here.

[*Enter* JIM *following him.*]

Jim. Yes, Massa, we's heah!

Andrews. And who are you?

Jon. *   *   My grandfather fit and died in the Rev—

Andrews. Never mind your grandfather now; where are you from?

Jon. *   *   In the shake of a lamb's tail.

Andrews. Thank heavens? Three cheers for General Corse. [*The men cheer.*] Did you see anything of the enemy?

Jon. *   *   Fightin' 'em for the last two hours.

Jim. Yes sah, Massa, we seed acres of 'em, acres of 'em —millions.

Andrews. Where?

Jim. We've jest done left 'em, Massa. Ise been among 'em all day. Ise been scoutin' I has; de General told me to find out all I could, and Ise jest done left 'em.

Andrews. How many are there?

Jim. Oh! Massa, de woods is full of 'em—de woods is full chuck up.

Andrews. Have they any big guns?

Jim. De guns wid de cartwheels on em, Massa? Thousands ob 'em.

Andrews. Did you hear them fire?

Jim. Golly, Massa, I guess I has; it was only a little while ago, and I heerd one of dem tings going fro de air. As it went over my head it hollered out jest as if it was inquiring for me [*imitating a shell*] whar is ye? whar is ye? and just cause it couldn't find me it got mad and busted itself a little furder on. [*They laugh.*]

Andrews. Rifled artillery—hark! [*Cheers are heard at* L.] Here comes Corse! [*Men all cheer.*]

Men. Where? where?

Jon. * * Here he is! here he is!

[*Enter* CORSE, *men with colors, etc.*—ANDREWS *and* CORSE *shake hands—Enter* LOTTIE *and* MAY, GRAVES *and* HOWE—*all enter at* L. 1 E.]

Corse. Colonel, here are two ladies who have placed themselves under my protection. Please see that they have a safe and secure place till the battle is over. [*To* GRAVES *and* HOWE.] Gentlemen, do you still keep your parole?

Graves. I will. General.

Howe. I will not. You are surrounded here in this mountain, not by a rebel mob, but by Hood's whole army. You cannot hold this place five minutes against his gallant soldiers. Before the sun goes down I shall be free and you shall take my place.

Corse. There will be a heap of dead rebels first.

Jon. * * The old man's true blue!

Jim. [*Imitating* JONATHAN, *jumps up, etc.*] Hoora, we is true blue, we is!

Howe. Black, you mean, you dirty nigger.

Jim. Look heah, sah, who you callin' nigger. [*Approaches him.*]

Corse. Stop, Jim, stop.

Jim. Ise a free nigger, I is, and I 'lows no white trash to call me nigger. [*Men jeer* HOWE.]

Corse. Remember, men, these are prisoners of war and must not be insulted. Colonel, escort these ladies to some place of safety. [*Exit Col.* ANDREWS, MAY *and* LOTTIE,] [*To* GRAVES.] Doctor, I accept your parole. [*To* JONATHAN.] Jonathan, take charge of your prisoner; if he attempts to escape, shoot him. [*Exit* HOWE *under charge of* JONATHAN. CORSE *looks towards Kenesaw with his glass.*]

Bell. General, not a mile away, off to the right, come some of Kilpatrick's cavalry, and a party of rebels are trying to intercept them.

Corse. [*Springing on the works—looks through his glass down the mountain.*] 'Tis Colonel Estes! he will be killed or captured now certain. There he comes! he cannot avoid them! he must fight. Oh! if I could only help him.

Bell. They have formed a line in his front.

Corse. Yes, but, by heavens! he has charged through them. Here he comes! here he comes! Gallant fellow! [*Cheering off stage at* L. *Enter* ESTES, *covered with mud and battle-worn—exhausted, he embraces* CORSE.] Well done, my gallant boy, well done.

[*Enter* LOTTIE *followed by* JIM R. 1 E. ESTES *embraces* LOTTIE.]

Lottie. Thank God! Harry, you are safe. I saw it all from yonder rock. My brave, my gallant Harry!

Estes. *   *   Where will you go?

Lottie. Oh! I am safe, 'tis only for you I fear.

Bell. The enemy is moving.

[*Shouts off the stage, "Here they come!"—the men kneel and bring their muskets to a ready.*]

Corse. Silence! Let no man speak or fire until I give the word. Miss Howe, you had better retire at once. LOTTIE *shakes hands with* ESTES *and exits* R. 1 E.] Comrades, we are soldiers here from Ohio, Minnesota, Iowa, Wisconsin, and Illinois; we must surrender or fight as we never fought before. I will not deceive you--we are less than two thousand strong, and the enemy six times that number. We cannot surrender—then let us fight, and may God defend the right! [*Cheers as if the line extended off the stage at* R. *and* L.] Now lay for them and let no man fire a single shot till I give the word. Estes, go to the right and watch for my signal. [ESTES *exit* L. 1 E.] Now, men, steady. Here they come!

[*Rebel orders are heard in the distance on the right and in the front given by* HOWE: "*Forward, men! Move straight to the front! Steady on the right!—a pause—a voice very close—"Where are ye, Yanks! Where are ye Yanks!"*]

Corse. [*Springing up.*] Here we are! Fire! Fire! Give

it to 'em! [CORSE *falls with a head wound*. JONATHAN
*catches him in his arms and eases him down; sets him against
knoll on which signal officer was standing. Rebels retreat—
firing ceases.*] [*Enter* ESTES L. 2 E.]
Estes. Is he dead?
Corse. No, I'm worth a hundred dead men yet and I'll
defend this post. [*They bind up his head.*]
Bell. A signal on Kenesaw! See it? [*A small light is
seen on the mountain.*]
Corse. What does he say?
Bell. [*Reads very slowly.*] Hold—on—do—not—give—
up—we—are—coming—to—your—aid —Howard—is—with-
in—five—miles—with—his—whole—corps—SHERMAN.
Corse. Signal back : We—have—repulsed—them—once
—half—my—head—is— gone—but—we— will—hold—the—
fort—or—die. [*To* ESTES.] Take command, Estes. I'm
faint. [*Faints away.*]
Bell. Colonel, they are coming again.
Estes. *   *   Contract his lines and refuse——
Jon. He is dead, sir.
Estes. Well, Lieutenant Colonel Wharton——
Jon. Badly wounded; so is the Major.
Estes. *   *   Who led the last attack?
Bell. Yes, sir, and there he comes leading as before.
Estes. [Has he escaped?
[*Exit* JIM *in haste and return. . .*
Jim. [*Excited enter* R. 2 E.] He's done gone suah, Mas-
sa, dead sartin.
Estes. *   *   Men, ready, fire! [*Firing on both sides
for short time—rebels show themselves and two or three fall
dead—*HOWE *rushes at* ESTES—*they cross swords and fight —*
CORSE *revives and starts up—sees* HOWE, *draws pistol and
fires—*HOWE *falls dead; when* HOWE *falls firing ceases, rebels retreat—enter* MAY *and kneels over* HOWE; LOTTIE *rushes to* ESTES, *they embrace and stand in a picture, soldiers all
kneel. Tableau, decoration of soldiers' graves on platform
in background.*]

[CURTAIN.]

ACT VI.

SCENE 4.

Interior of Squire DUNHAM's *house in Vermont—Mrs.* D. *and* LOTTIE ESTES *seated at table* C.

[*Enter Squire* R. 2 E.]

Mrs. Dunham. Well, father, what is the news this morning? I am very anxious to learn. Ever since that terrible battle of Allatoona I have had such a terrible anxiety for our son Harry.

Squire D. Well, mother, I have heard nothing definite. Mariar Bunker was over this morning to borrow a hoe, and said something about the people in the village being very excited about some late news, but was in a hurry and didn't stop to learn the nature of their excitement. I sent that rascal Jim to town over an hour ago for our mail but he has not returned yet. I suppose he has got in with that darkey Captain Harkness brought home with him and they are exchanging war yarns. [*To* LOTTIE.] Lottie, what was it Harry had to say about Richmond in that letter you got the other day?

Lottie. I have the letter in my pocket, father. I'll read it to you. [LOTTIE *takes letter out of her pocket and reads.*]

BEFORE RICHMOND,{
April 7, 1865,{

My Dear Wife:—Since my last letter there has been but little change in matters here. We still keep up our skirmishing, and I think the rebels are weakening. One of our spies came in this morning and reports that the rebels cannot possibly hold out more than two days at the outside. Richmond is the stronghold of the Southern Confederacy and when that falls their hopes are gone. Our boys are all in good spirits and are confident of success. We all look anxiously forward to the day when we can come home to our dear friends and live in peace and retirement from all scenes of strife and warfare. God grant that that day is close at hand. Jonathan Bunker has been over to see me this morning and wants you to tell Mariar for him, to not worry about him for he is as sound as a brick and will be ready to go to Congress in less than a year. He is the same old sixpence and keeps the whole regiment in good spirits with his comicalities. I have just received an order to report to General Buckland's headquarters so I will have to stop writing for this time. Keep up a brave

heart. Give my best to father and mother. Tell them I
will be with them before long if God spares me.
Your loving, HARRY.

Mrs. D. Brave Harry! I believe if he was to have an
opportunity to write while in the midst of a battle He
would be just as cool and resolute as if at home.

Squire D. Yes, mother, we have just cause to feel proud
of our noble son, and I could not think more of him if he
was our own boy.

Mrs. D. Lottie, won't you sing for us that song you
sang last evening, "Just before the Battle, Mother"?

Lottie. Yes, mother, I will try; it is very good and I
think appropriate after reading Harry's letter.

[LOTTIE *sings "Just before the Battle, Mother."—invisible chorus outside—at close of chorus* JIM *is heard
singing, "Johnny fill up the bowl," at* R. 2 E.]

Squire D. There comes the rascal, Jim, now. About
time I should think. He's a spoiled chicken sure.

[*Enter* JIM *singing, stops, looks at Squire D., laughing
and dancing.*]

Jim. Bully for Corse! bully for Grant! hurrah for Pil-
katrick! de war am done busted suah. [*Laughs, etc.*]

Squire D. Jim, you rascal, what is the matter of you?
Have you taken leave of what little sense you ever had?
Come here, sir.

Jim. Oh! Massa Dunham, go 'way, now. You don't
know nuffin about it. You jest ought to been down town
an' heerd de fuss dey's makin' down dar. Golly! flags
flyin', drums beatin' and boys hollerin' and I don't know
what all. Everybody's crazy, so I jist got crazy too.

Squire D. Well, I should say you had. Come here and
give me my papers and then see if you can keep quiet until I see what this fuss is about.

Jim. [*Feeling for the papers.*] Oh! Ise a quiet nigger,
I is.

Squire D. Well! well! hurry up and give me the papers. I'm in a hurry.

Jim. Yas. [*Aside.*] So be I in a hurry. [*Going through
his clothes lively.*] Now, whar's dem papers.

Squire D. [*Impatiently.*] Come, come, Jim, be lively.

Jim. Yes, Massa. [*Finds paper in his hat.* *Aside.*] Paper been up. [*To D.*] Daa's your paper, and now look heah, Missus Dunham, you and Missus Lottie better yet ready to hold him for when he reads dat paper he's gwine to tear round I tell you. case dere's mighty good news in dar. [*Hands paper to* DUNHAM.]

Squire D. [*Takes paper and reads—jumps up excitedly—* JIM *falls down and rolls over two or three times, etc.*] Hoora! h·ora! hip! hip! the best news I ever hearn.

Mrs. D. Why, father, how you act. What's the matter?

Squire D. Why, mother, the best news you ever heard. Listen: Richmond has fallen, Lee has surrendered to Grant, and now the war will be over and our boy will be home again.

Jim. [*Aside.*] I guess Massa Dunham mighty near leavin' his senses too. I knowed it would fotch him.

Squire D. Jim, come here now; go over and tell Mrs. Bunker to come over I wish to see her.

Jim. All right, Massa. [*Exit L. 2 E.*]

Squire D. Mother, it will not be long now until our boys return and we must be making preparations for a reception. I have sent for Mrs. Bunker and you women folks can fix your plans for cooking and I will see to the outdoor work.

Mrs. D. Yes, father, Lottie has been very anxious to show me what she can do and now she shall have a chance.

Lottie. That I will, mother, and you shall see that I can work too. [*Enter* MARIAR *and* JIM L. 2 E.*]

Mariar. Good morning, folks. Squire, did you get your paper?

Squire D. Yes, Mrs. Bunker and the war will be over now soon, and Jonathan will be home before you know it. [*Knock at door* L. 2 E.] Jim, go to the door and see who's knocking. [*Enter* JONATHAN *in a rush·*]

Jon. I'm here. [*All start up surprised.* MARIA *goes to him—they embrace.*]

All. Jonathan!

Squire D. Why, Jonathan, I did not expect you so soon. We just heard of the surrender of Lee but had no idea that you would be home so soon.

Jon. * * Six o'clock train. So you see I'm here.

Lottie. Thank God.

Squire D. Home at six o'clock, eh? Well, we must manage to receive them. Jim, come here you rascal and stop that grinning. I've got work for you the rest of the day. [JIM *making motions as if blowing up his muscle.*] I want you to go and fix up that picnic table on the lawn; then go to the lumber yard and order one hundred feet of inch boards and we will extend it. After you have that done go down into the cellar and roll up two of the best barrels of cider, and be careful that you don't drink too much when you sample it.

Jim. [*Measuring about two inches on his fingers.*] Oh! no, massa, I don't drink much.

Mrs. D. Well, Jonathan, I'm glad to see you looking so well, and how thankful I am that this cruel war is over.

Jon. * * See how the old shanty looks.

Squire D. Well, Jonathan, you and Mariar be over when the boys come, and we will have a jolly time.

Jon. All right, Squire; come Mariar. [*Exit* JONATHAN *and* MARIAR R. 2 E.]

Squire D. Well now, Jim, what did I tell you to do? I bet you have forgotten.

Jim. Oh! no I aint, Massa. [*Scratches his head.*]

Squire D. Well, what was it?

Jim. You tole me to bring de lumber yard over on de lawn and put two barrels of cider on de nicpic table——

Squire D. Nonsense, blockhead! I told you nothing of the kind. But never mind, I'll go with you. [*To the ladies.*] Now, mother, you and Lottie work lively for the time is short——

Jim. Hoora! hoora! jest wait a minute. [*Throws up his hat. They all start. Enter Colonel* ESTES, *throws his sword on the floor, embraces* LOTTIE *and kisses her, shakes hands with Squire* D., *then with Mrs.* D.]

Squire D. Why, Harry, how's this? We did not expect you until six o'clock.

Estes. *   * I want you all to go with me.

Squire D. All right, Harry, my boy, we will all go. Mother, you and Lottie get on your things and be ready to start at once.

[*Scene closes.*]

SCENE II.

Exterior. *Bummer march, first soldiers march across stage, rout step—band plays, "Johnny comes marching home. Soldiers pass around and march in again, headed by Colonel* ESTES, *Captain* HARKNESS, *officers, etc.—band plays "Yankee Doodle"—march off at* R. *and form for Tableau.*

SCENE III.

Surrender of Lee. Tableaux on platform.

[CURTAIN.]

THE END.

www.ingramcontent.com/pod-product-compliance
Lightning Source LLC
Chambersburg PA
CBHW031800090426
42739CB00008B/1099